GABRIEL JACKSON

THE PASSION OF OUR LORD JESUS CHRIST

for soprano and tenor soloists, SATB, and ten players

VOCAL SCORE

OXFORD

UNIVERSITY PRESS

Commissioned by the Warden and Fellows of Merton College, Oxford, to celebrate the 750th Anniversary of the foundation of the college

First performed by Emma Tring (soprano), Nick Pritchard (tenor), the Choir of Merton College, Oxford, and the Oxford Contemporary Sinfonia, conducted by Benjamin Nicholas, at Merton College on 4 April 2014

Duration: 60 minutes

TEXTS

1. Palm Sunday

> *Vexilla regis prodeunt,*
> *fulget crucis mysterium,*
> *quo carne carnis conditor*
> *suspensus est patibulo.*

Tell ye the daughter of Sion, Behold, thy King cometh unto thee, meek, and sitting upon an ass, and a colt the foal of an ass. *(Matthew 21.5)*

Hosanna to the son of David: Blessed is he that cometh in the name of the Lord; Hosanna in the highest.

And when Jesus was come into Jerusalem, all the city was moved, saying, Who is this? And the multitude said, This is Jesus the prophet of Nazareth of Galilee. *(Matthew 21.9b–11)*

> *Vexilla regis prodeunt,*
> *fulget crucis mysterium,*
> *quo carne carnis conditor*
> *suspensus est patibulo.*

> Venantius Fortunatus (c.530–c.600/609)
> (Hymn at Vespers, Passiontide)*

*English translation:
The banners of the king advance,
the mystery of the cross shines forth,
the creator of all flesh, flesh himself,
is hung from the gallows.

2. Anointing at Bethany

> Almighty God, Father of all mercies,
> we thine unworthy servants
> do give thee most humble and hearty thanks
> for all thy goodness and loving-kindness
> to us and to all men.

Behold, a woman in the city, which was a sinner, when she knew that Jesus sat at meat in Simon the Pharisees house, brought an alabaster box of ointment,
And stood at his feet behind him weeping, and began to wash his feet with tears, and did wipe them with the hairs of her head, and kissed his feet, and anointed them with the ointment. *(Luke 7.37–38)*

> We bless thee for our creation, preservation,
> and all the blessings of this life;
> but above all for thine inestimable love
> in the redemption of the world by our Lord Jesus Christ;
> for the means of grace, and for the hope of glory.

And he turned to the woman, and said unto Simon, Seest thou this woman? I entered into thine house, thou gavest me no water for my feet: but she hath washed my feet with tears, and wiped them with the hairs of her head. *(Luke 7.44–45)*

Wherefore I say unto thee, Her sins, which are many, are forgiven; for she loved much: but to whom

little is forgiven, the same loveth little.
And he said unto her, Thy sins are forgiven. *(Luke 7.47–48)*

> And, we beseech thee,
> give us that due sense of all thy mercies,
> that our hearts may be unfeignedly thankful;
> and that we show forth thy praise,
> not only with our lips, but in our lives,
> by giving up ourselves to thy service,
> and by walking before thee
> in holiness and righteousness all our days;

And they that sat at meat with him began to say within themselves, Who is this that forgiveth sins also? *(Luke 7.49)*

> through Jesus Christ our Lord,
> to whom, with thee and the Holy Spirit,
> be all honour and glory, world without end. Amen.

> *The General Thanksgiving*
> Edward Reynolds (1599–1676)
> (Warden of Merton College, Oxford, 1660–1661)

And he said to the woman, Thy faith hath saved thee; go in peace. *(Luke 7.50)*

3.   Last Supper and Footwashing

Ave, verum corpus natum
de Maria Virgine,

Now when the even was come, Jesus sat down with the twelve. (Matthew 26.20)

Vere passum immolatum
in Cruce pro homine,

And as they were eating, Jesus took bread, and blessed it, and brake it, and gave it to the disciples, and said, Take, eat; this is my body.
And he took the cup, and gave thanks, and gave it to them, saying, Drink ye all of it;
For this is my blood of the new testament, which is shed for many for the remission of sins. *(Matthew 26.26–28)*

> *Ubi caritas et amor, Deus ibi est.*
> *Congregavit nos in unum Christi amor.*

Supper being ended, the devil having now put into the heart of Judas Iscariot, Simons son, to betray him; *(John 13.2)*

Cujus latus perforatum
unda fluxit sanguine,

Jesus riseth from supper, and laid aside his garments; and took a towel, and girded himself. *(John 13.4)*

Esto nobis praegustatum
in mortis examine.

After that he poureth water into a bason, and began to wash the disciples feet, and to wipe them with the towel wherewith he was girded. *(John 13.5)*

After he had washed their feet, he said unto them, Know ye what I have done to you?
Ye call me Master and Lord: and ye say well; for so I am.
If I then, your Lord and Master, have washed your feet; ye also ought to wash one anothers feet.
For I have given you an example, that ye should do as I have done to you. *(John 13.12–15)*

Exultemus, et in ipso jucundemur.
Timeamus, et amemus Deum vivum
Et ex corde diligamus nos sincero.
Ubi caritas et amor, Deus ibi est.

Author unknown
(Antiphon during the Washing of the
Feet and Vespers on Maundy Thursday)**

Jesus was troubled in spirit, and said, Verily, verily, I say unto you, that one of you shall betray me.
Then the disciples looked one on another, doubting of whom he spake.
Now there was leaning on Jesus bosom one of his disciples, whom Jesus loved.
Simon Peter therefore beckoned to him, that he should ask who it should be of whom he spake.
He then lying on Jesus breast saith unto him, Lord, who is it?
Jesus answered, He it is, to whom I shall give a sop, when I have dipped it. And when he had dipped the sop, he gave it to Judas Iscariot, the son of Simon.
And after the sop Satan entered into him. *(John 13.21–27)*

O dulcis, O pie, O Jesu, Fili Mariae.

attrib. Pope Innocent VI (d.1362)
(Hymn to the Blessed Sacrament, Corpus Christi)*

Then said Jesus unto him, That thou doest, do quickly. He then having received the sop went immediately out: and it was night. *(John 13.30)*

*English translation:
Hail true body, born
of the Virgin Mary,
Who having truly suffered, was sacrificed
on the Cross for mankind,
Whose pierced side
flowed with water and blood,
May it be for us a foretaste [of heaven]
in the trial of death.
O sweet, O pious, O Jesus, Son of Mary.

**English translation:
Where charity and love are, God is there.
The love of Christ has gathered us into one.
Let us rejoice and delight in him.
Let us fear, and love, the living God
And may we love each other with a sincere heart.
Where charity and love are, God is there

4.   Gethsemane

Then cometh Jesus with them unto a place called Gethsemane, and saith unto the disciples, Sit ye here, while I go and pray yonder. *(Matthew 26.36)*

Such surge of black wings saw I never homing
Fast from a winter day's pale-gilt entombing
        Nor can the continent's entire woodland house them.
So many throats of known and unknown runnels
Shooting from thorny cliffs or poured through tunnels
        I never heard. Such rainstorm to arouse them
We in these parts yet bore not in such torrents,
Nor warring winds enraged to abhorrence;
        The sun was laughed to scorn, his god-head pelted
With sharp bones wrenched from sylvan nature; flamed then
A lightning such, all other lightning (tamed then)
        Might be as honey, or kind balms slow-melted.

Then this sad evening, this echo of existence,
And what was near driven to enormous distance.

The Evil Hour
Edmund Blunden (1896–1974)
(Fellow of Merton College, Oxford, 1931–1944)

While he yet spake, lo, Judas, one of the twelve, came, and with him a great multitude with swords
and staves, from the chief priests and elders of the people. *(Matthew 26.47)*

> – I am only the phrase
> Of an unknown musician;
> By a gentle voice spoken
> I stole forth and met you
> In halcyon days.
> Yet, frail as I am, you yourself shall be broken
> Before we are parted; I have but one mission:
> Till death to beset you.

Now he that betrayed him gave them a sign, saying, Whomsoever I shall kiss, that same is he: hold
him fast.
And forthwith he came to Jesus, and said, Hail, master; and kissed him. *(Matthew 26.48–49)*

> – You phantoms, pursue me,
> Be upon me, amaze me,
> Though nigh all your presence
> With sorrow enchant me,
> With sorrow renew me!
> Songless and gleamless I near no new pleasance,
> In subtle returnings of ecstasy raise me,
> To my winding-sheet haunt me!

from *Intimations of Mortality*
Edmund Blunden
(Used by permission of the Author's estate)

5.   Caiaphas, Peter and Pilate

They led Jesus away to the high priest: and with him were assembled all the chief priests and the
elders and the scribes.
And Peter followed him afar off, even into the palace of the high priest: and he sat with the servants,
and warmed himself at the fire.
And the chief priests and all the council sought for witness against Jesus to put him to death; and
found none. *(Mark 14.53–55)*

> Sitting by the streames that glide
> Downe by Babell's towring wall,
> With our tears wee filde the tyde,
> Whilst our myndfull thoughts recall
> Thee, O Sion, and thy fall.

As Peter was beneath in the palace, there cometh one of the maids of the high priest:
And when she saw Peter warming himself, she looked upon him, and said, And thou also wast
with Jesus of Nazareth.
But he denied, saying, I know not, neither understand I what thou sayest. And he went out into the
porch; and the cock crew.
And a maid saw him again, and began to say to them that stood by, This is one of them.
And he denied it again. And a little after, they that stood by said again to Peter, Surely thou art one

of them: for thou art a Galilaean, and thy speech agreeth thereto.

But he began to curse and to swear, saying, I know not this man of whom ye speak.

And the second time the cock crew. And Peter called to mind the word that Jesus said unto him, Before the cock crow twice, thou shalt deny me thrice. And when he thought thereon, he wept. *(Mark 14.69–72)*

> Our neglected harps unstrung,
> Not acquainted with the hand
> Of the skillfull tuner, hunge
> On the willow trees that stand
> Planted in the neighbour land.

In the morning the chief priests held a consultation with the elders and scribes and the whole council, and bound Jesus, and carried him away, and delivered him to Pilate.

And Pilate asked him, Art thou the King of the Jews? And he answering said unto them, Thou sayest it.

And the chief priests accused him of many things: but he answered nothing.

And Pilate asked him again, saying, Answerest thou nothing? behold how many things they witness against thee.

But Jesus yet answered nothing; so that Pilate marvelled. *(Mark 15.1–5)*

> Yet the spightfull foe commands
> Songs of mirthe, and bids us lay
> To dumb harps our captive hands,
> And to scoffe our sorrowes, say,
> Sing us some sweet Hebrewe lay.

Now at that feast he released unto them one prisoner, whomsoever they desired.

And there was one named Barabbas, which lay bound with them that had made insurrection with him, who had committed murder in the insurrection.

And the multitude crying aloud began to desire him to do as he had ever done unto them.

But Pilate answered them, saying, Will ye that I release unto you the King of the Jews?

For he knew that the chief priests had delivered him for envy.

But the chief priests moved the people, that he should rather release Barabbas unto them.

And Pilate answered and said again unto them, What will ye then that I shall do unto him whom ye call the King of the Jews?

And they cried out again, Crucify him. *(Mark 15.6–13)*

> But, we say, our holye strayn
> Is too pure for heathen land,
> Nor may wee God's himmes prophane,
> Or move eyther voyce or hand
> To delight a savage band.

Then Pilate said unto them, Why, what evil hath he done? And they cried out the more exceedingly, Crucify him.

And so Pilate, willing to content the people, released Barabbas unto them, and delivered Jesus, when he had scourged him, to be crucified. *(Mark 15.14–15)*

> Holye Salem, if thy love
> Fall from my forgetfull harte,
> May the skill by which I move
> Strings of musicke, tun'd with art,
> From my withered hand departe.

> *Psalm 137*
> Thomas Carew (1595–1640)
> (Matriculated at Merton College, Oxford, 1608)

6. Crucifixion

And it was the third hour, and they crucified him.
And the superscription of his accusation was written over, THE KING OF THE JEWS.
And with him they crucify two thieves; the one on his right hand, and the other on his left.
And the scripture was fulfilled, which saith, And he was numbered with the transgressors.
And they that passed by railed on him, wagging their heads, and saying, Ah, thou that destroyest the temple, and buildest it in three days, Save thyself, and come down from the cross. Likewise also the chief priests mocking said among themselves with the scribes, He saved others; himself he cannot save. Let Christ the King of Israel descend now from the cross, that we may see and believe. And they that were crucified with him reviled him. *(Mark 15.23–32)*

> *Crux fidelis inter omnes arbor una nobilis:*
> *nulla silva talem profert fronde, flore, germine.*
> *Dulce lignum, dulces clavos, dulce pondus sustinet.*

And when the sixth hour was come, there was darkness over the whole land until the ninth hour.
And at the ninth hour Jesus cried with a loud voice, saying, Eloi, Eloi, lama sabachthani? which is, being interpreted, My God, my God, why hast thou forsaken me?
And some of them that stood by, when they heard it, said, Behold, he calleth Elias.
And one ran and filled a spunge full of vinegar, and put it on a reed, and gave him to drink, saying, Let alone; let us see whether Elias will come to take him down.
And Jesus cried with a loud voice, and gave up the ghost. *(Mark 15.33–37)*

> *Pange lingua gloriosi lauream certaminis,*
> *et super crucis trophaeo dic triumphum nobilem:*
> *qualiter Redemptor orbis immolatus vicerit.*

And the veil of the temple was rent in twain from the top to the bottom. And when the centurion, which stood over against him, saw that he so cried out, and gave up the ghost, he said, Truly this man was the Son of God. *(Mark 15.38–39)*

> *Aequa Patri Filioque, inclito Paraclito,*
> *sempiterna sit beatae Trinitati gloria,*
> *cuius alma nos redemit atque servat gratia. Amen.*

> Venantius Fortunatus (c.530–c.600/609)
> (Hymn at Matins, Passiontide)*

*English translation:
Cross of our faith, uniquely one noble tree:
no woodland can produce a tree to match in leaf, flower or seed.
Sweet is the wood that bears the sweet nails, the sweet burden.

Tell out my tongue, the victory in the glorious struggle,
and tell of the noble triumph in the victory of the cross:
how the world's Redeemer, through his sacrifice, has conquered.

Equally to the Father and the Son, and to the glorious Paraclete,
eternal glory be to the blessed Trinity,
whose loving grace has redeemed and saved us. Amen

7. The End and the Beginning

What we call the beginning is often the end
And to make an end is to make a beginning.
The end is where we start from. And every phrase
And sentence that is right (where every word is at home,
Taking its place to support the others,

The word neither diffident nor ostentatious,
An easy commerce of the old and the new,
The common word exact without vulgarity,
The formal word precise but not pedantic,
The complete consort dancing together)
Every phrase and every sentence is an end and a beginning,
Every poem an epitaph. And any action
Is a step to the block, to the fire, down the sea's throat
Or to an illegible stone: and that is where we start.
We die with the dying:
See, they depart, and we go with them.
We are born with the dead:
See, they return, and bring us with them.
The moment of the rose and the moment of the yew-tree
Are of equal duration. A people without history
Is not redeemed from time, for history is a pattern
Of timeless moments. So, while the light fails
On a winter's afternoon, in a secluded chapel
History is now and England.

With the drawing of this Love and the voice of this Calling

We shall not cease from exploration
And the end of all our exploring
Will be to arrive where we started
And know the place for the first time.
Through the unknown, remembered gate
When the last of earth left to discover
Is that which was the beginning;
At the source of the longest river
The voice of the hidden waterfall
And the children in the apple-tree
Not known, because not looked for
But heard, half-heard, in the stillness
Between two waves of the sea.
Quick now, here, now, always—
A condition of complete simplicity
(Costing not less than everything)
And all shall be well and
All manner of thing shall be well
When the tongues of flame are in-folded
Into the crowned knot of fire
And the fire and the rose are one.

from *Little Gidding*
T.S. Eliot (1888–1965)
(Graduate student at Merton College, Oxford, 1914–15)
(Used by permission of the Author's estate)

Libretto compiled by the Rev. Dr Simon Jones, Chaplain of Merton College, Oxford

The Passion of our Lord Jesus Christ

GABRIEL JACKSON

1. Palm Sunday

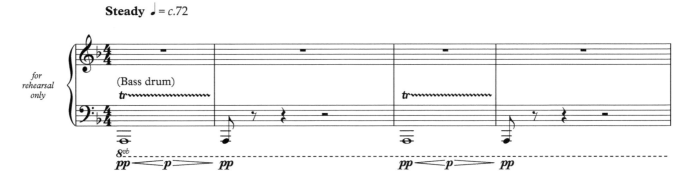

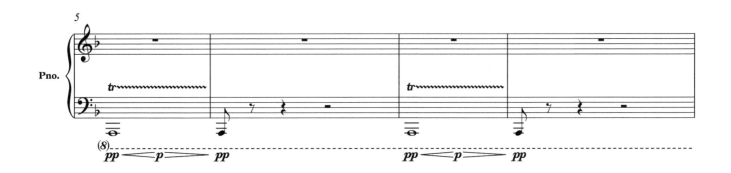

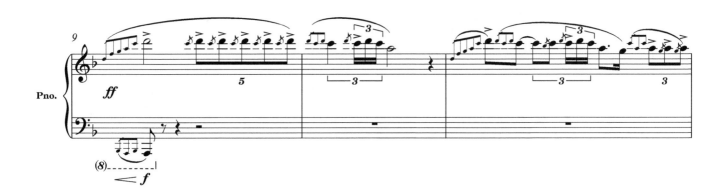

OXFORD UNIVERSITY PRESS, MUSIC DEPARTMENT, GREAT CLARENDON STREET, OXFORD OX2 6DP

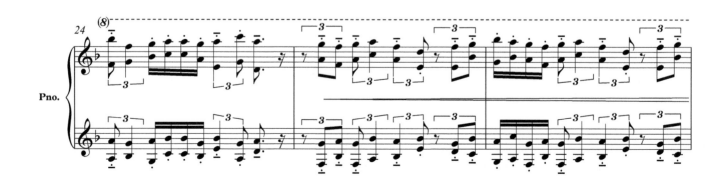

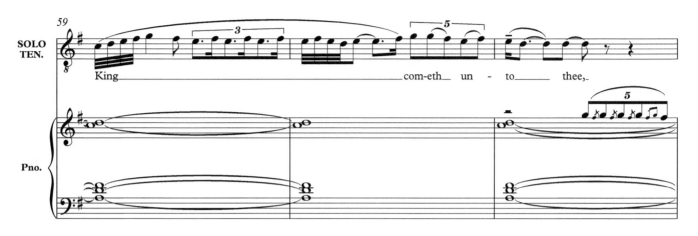

King_____ com-eth__ un - to_____ thee,__

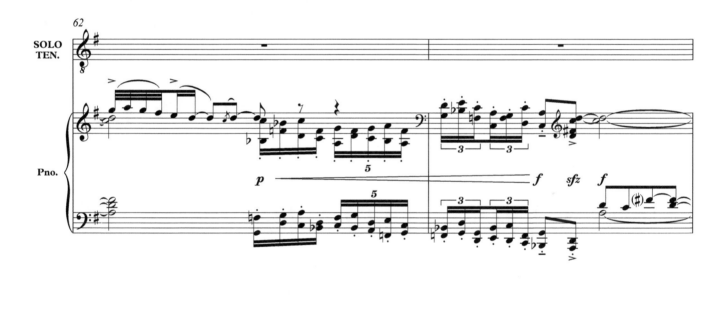

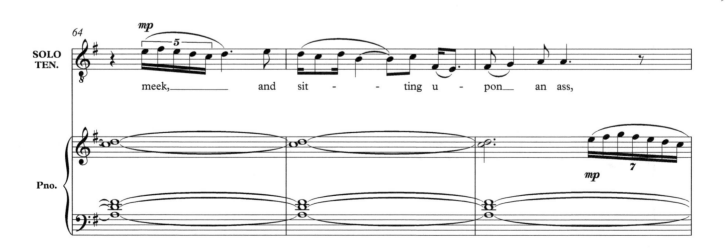

meek,_____ and sit - - ting u - pon an ass,

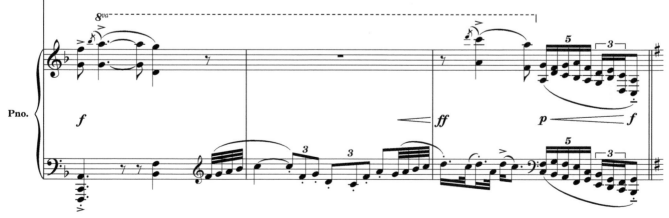

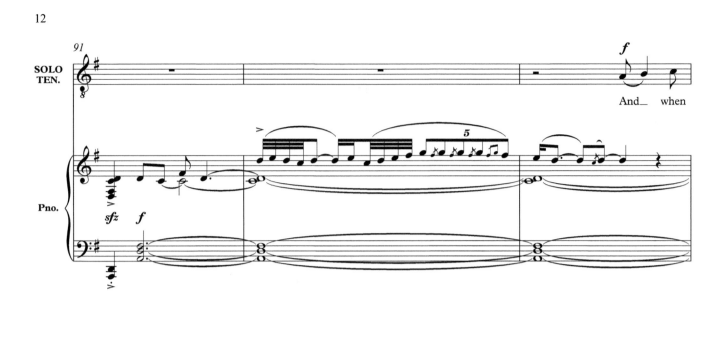

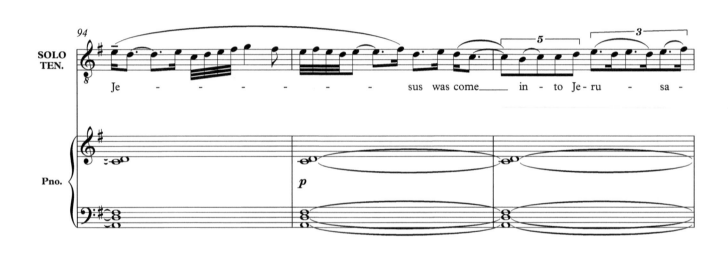

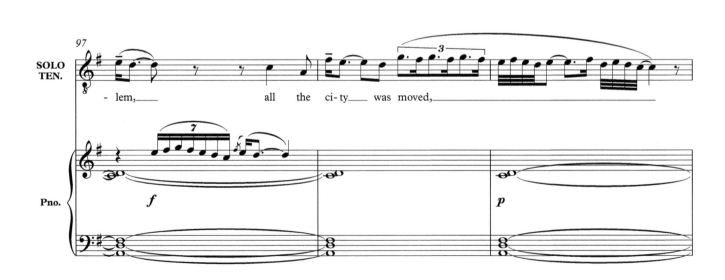

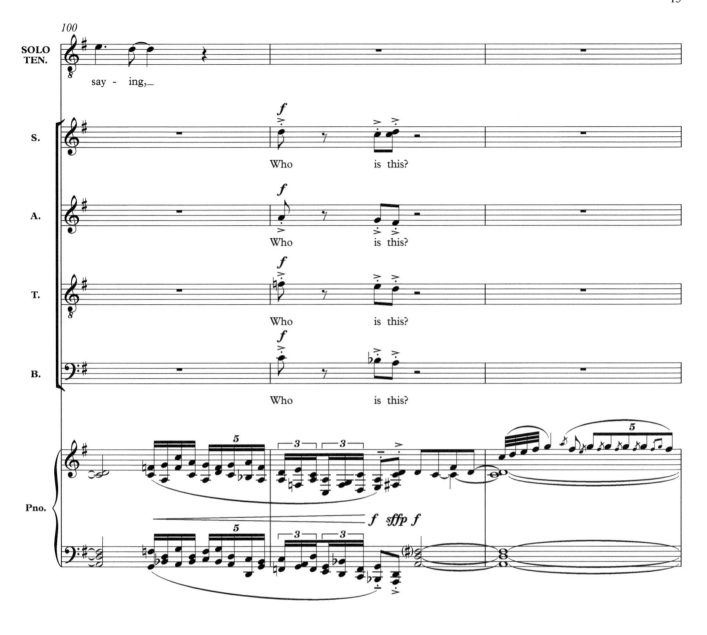

14

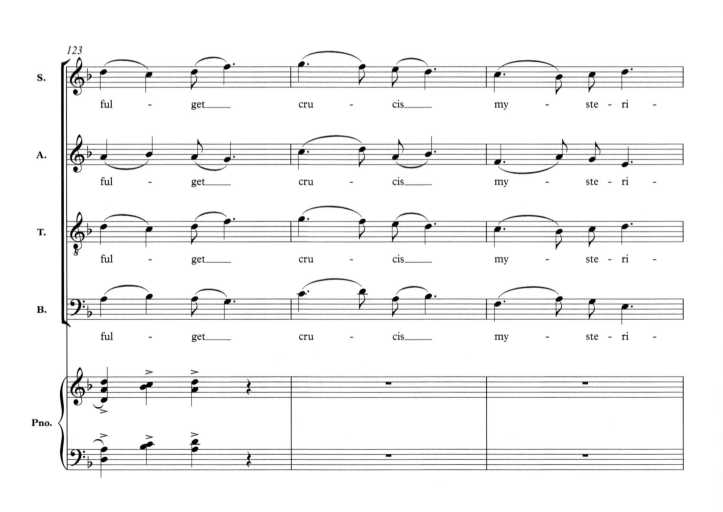

-pen - sus est___ pa - ti - bu - lo.___

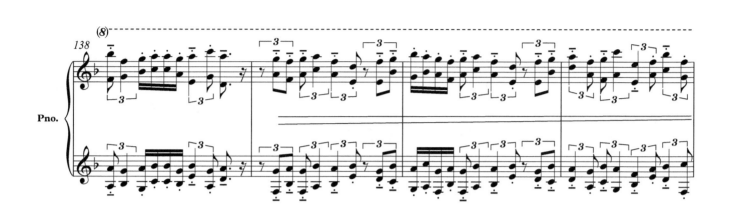

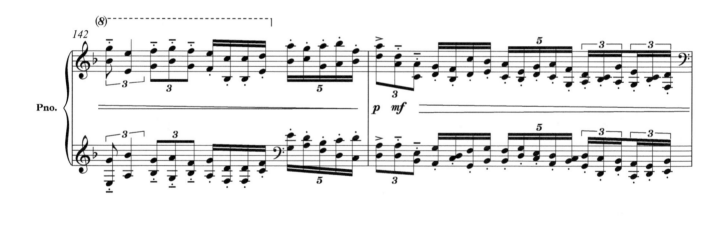

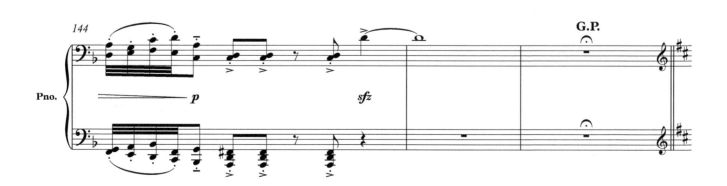

2. Anointing at Bethany

but to whom lit - tle is for - gi - ven, the same lov - eth lit - tle. And

And___ we be -

he said un - to her, Thy sins are for - gi - ven.

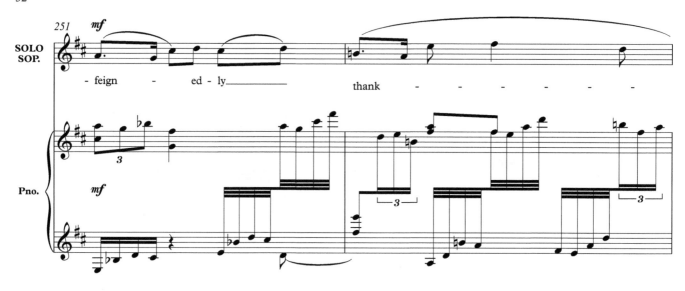

-feign - ed - ly_____ thank - - - - - -

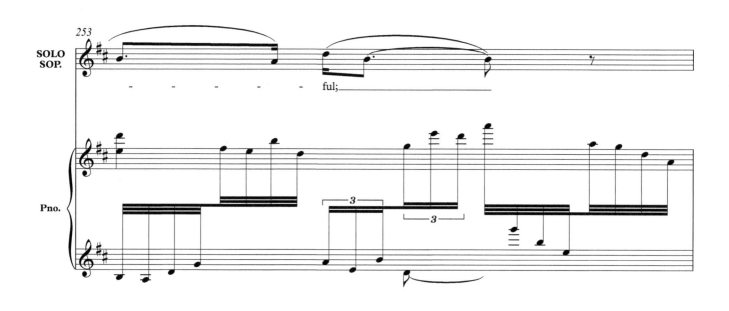

- - - - - ful;_____

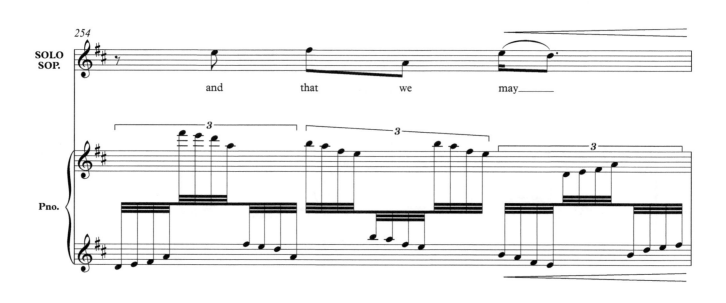

and that we may_____

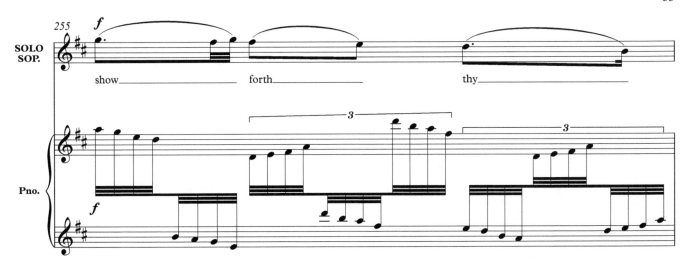

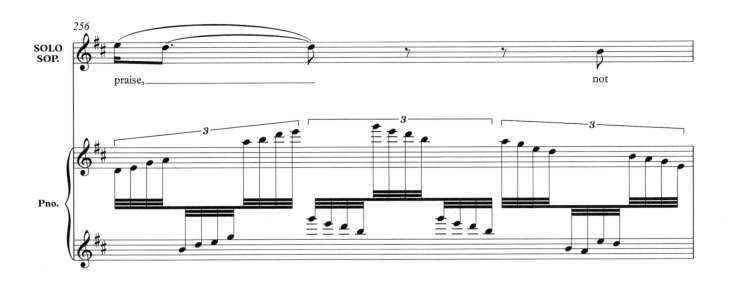

but in_____ our_____

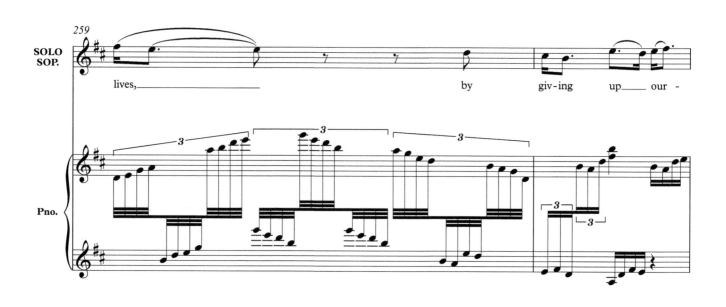

lives,_____ by giv-ing up____ our -

- selves_____ to thy ser - vice, and

by_____ walk - ing be - fore thee in ho - li - ness and

right - eous-ness all our days;_____

And they that sat at meat with him

And they that sat at meat with him

And they that sat at meat with him

And they that sat at meat with him

- nour and glo - - ry, world with-out

end. A - men.

And he said to the wo-man, Thy faith hath saved thee;

And he said to the wo-man, Thy faith hath saved thee;

And he said to the wo-man, Thy faith hath saved thee;

And he said to the wo-man, Thy faith hath saved thee;

go in peace.

go in peace.

go in peace.

go in peace.

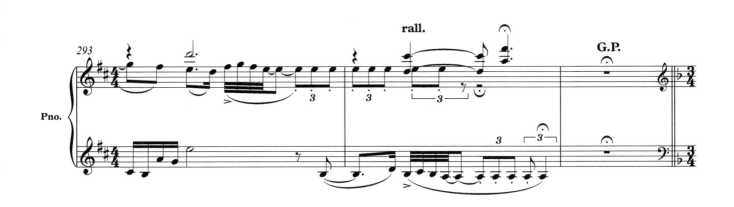

3. Last Supper and Footwashing

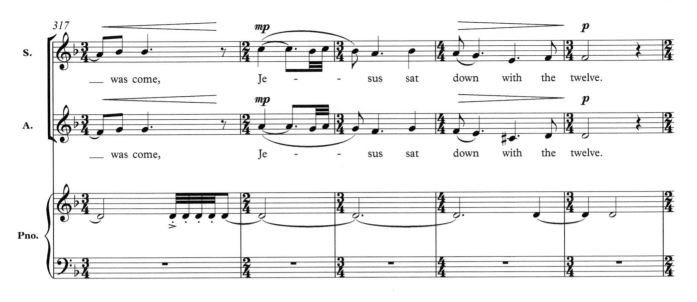

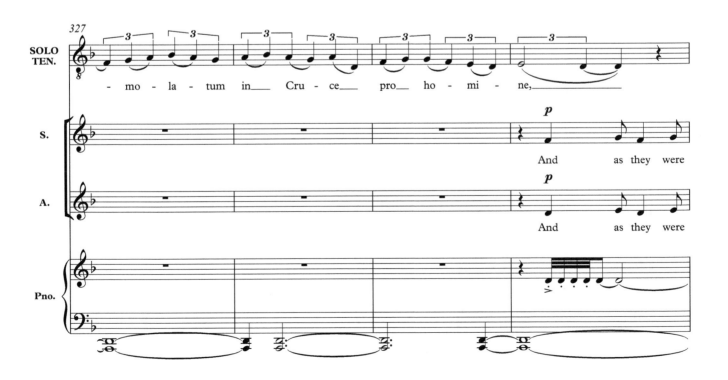

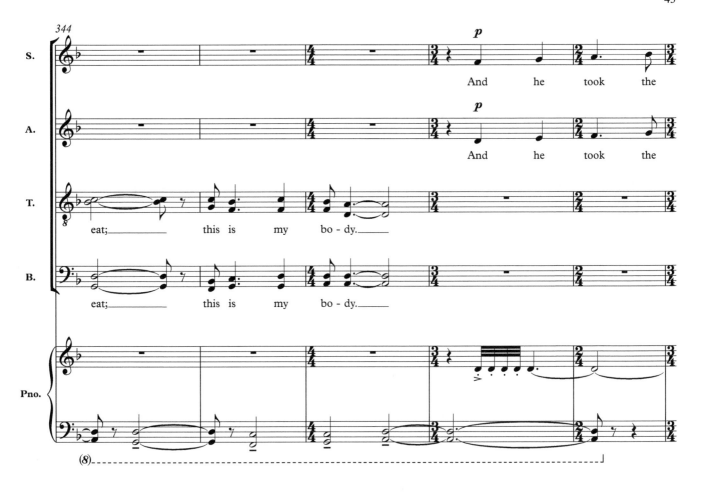

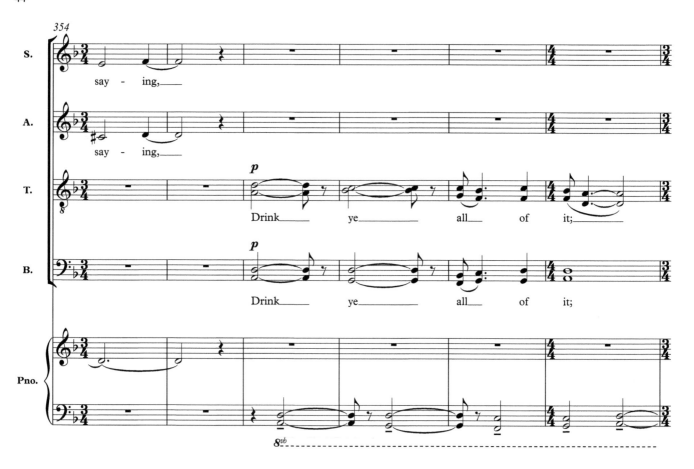

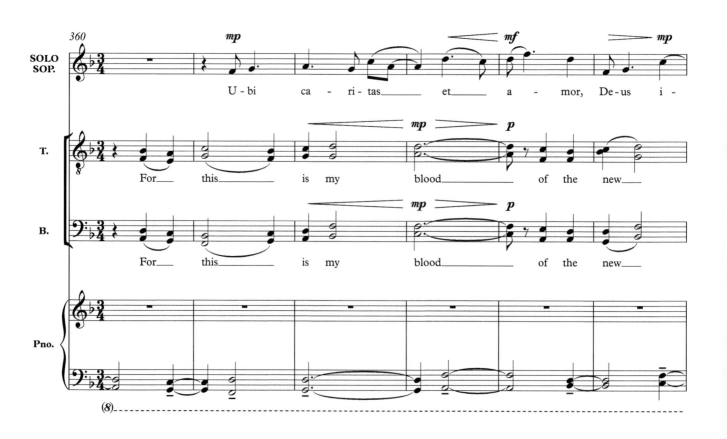

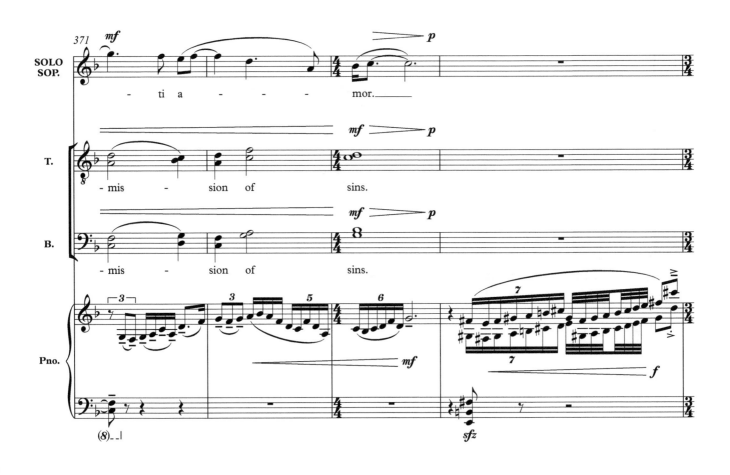

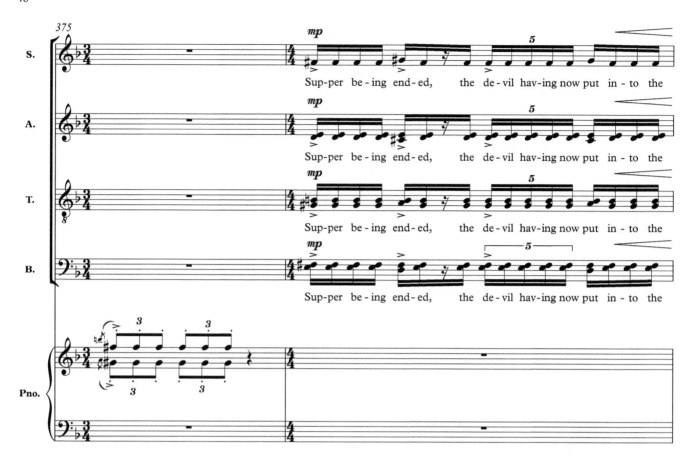

S. sup-per, and laid_____ a - side his gar-ments; and took____

A. sup-per, and laid_____ a - side his gar-ments; and took____

S. — a to-wel, and gird - ed him - self.

A. — a to-wel, and gird - ed him - self.

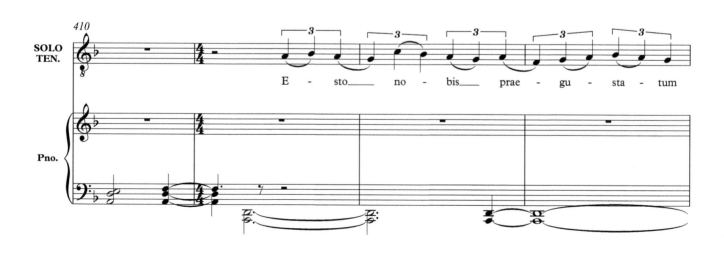

SOLO TEN. E - sto___ no - bis___ prae - gu - sta - tum

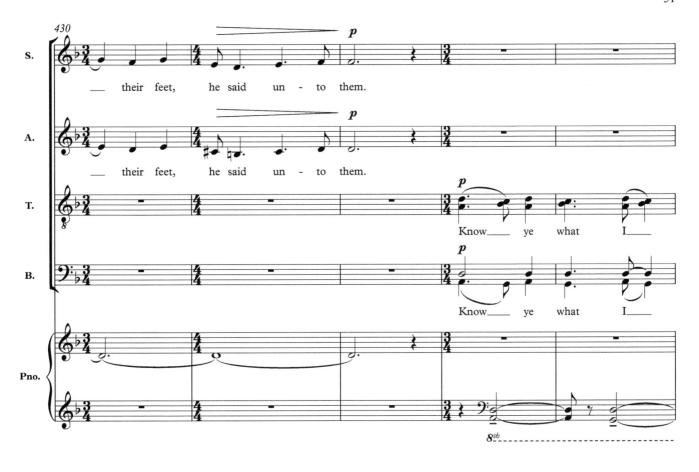

52

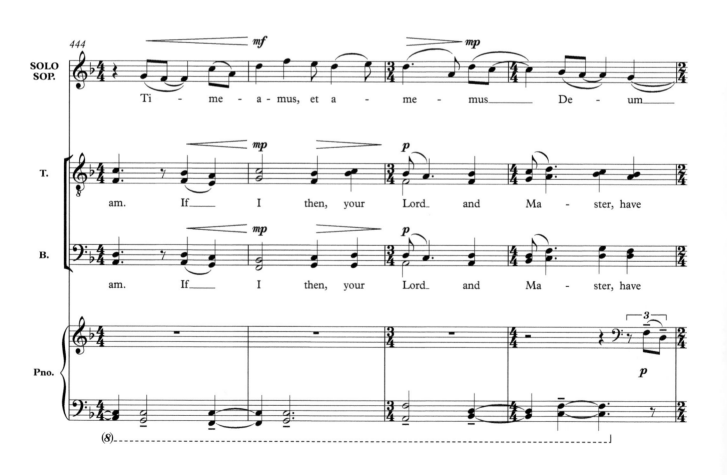

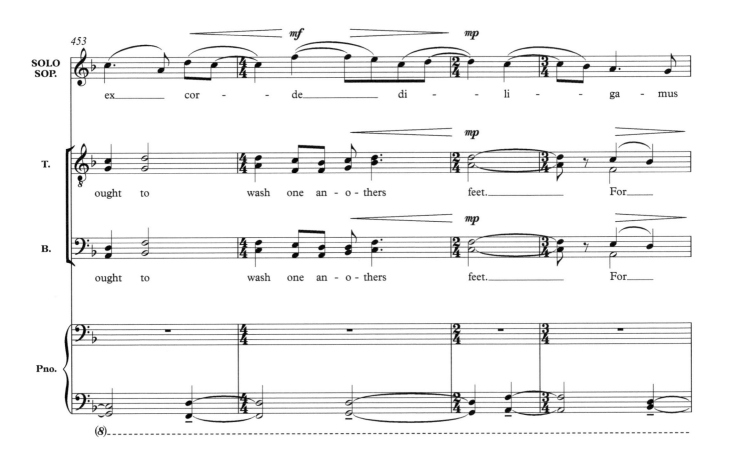

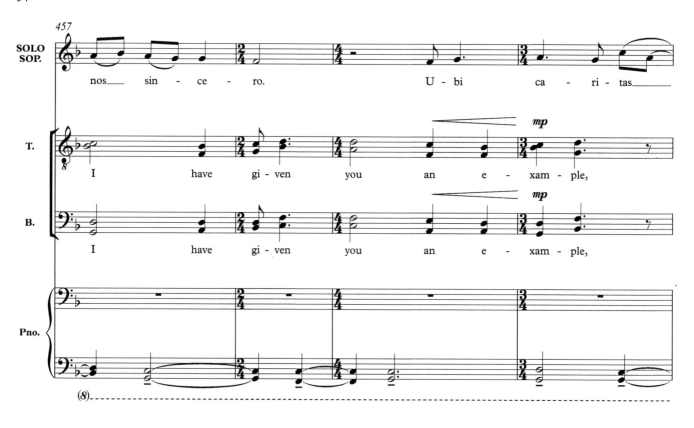

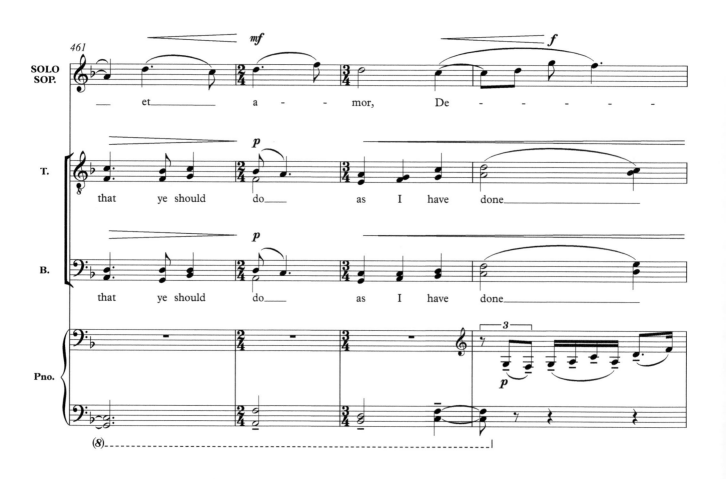

58

60

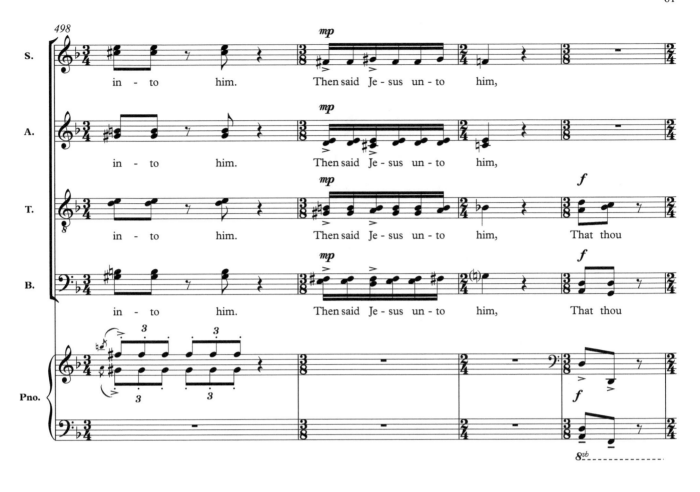

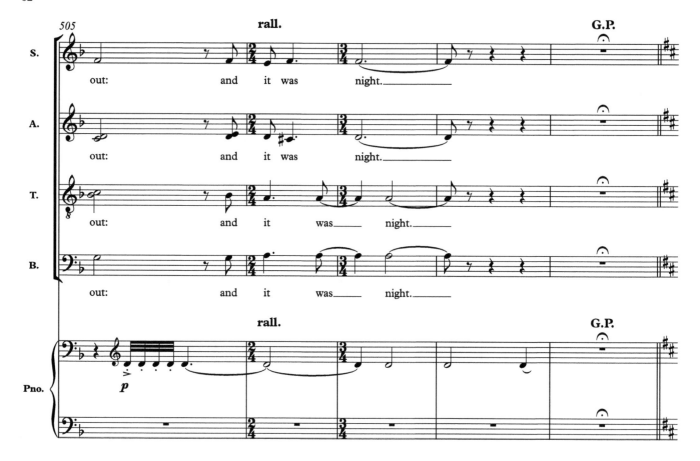

4. Gethsemane

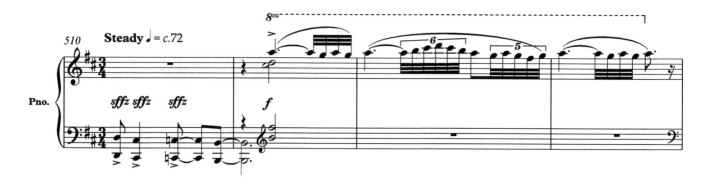

5. Caiaphas, Peter and Pilate

* pronounced "Babble's"

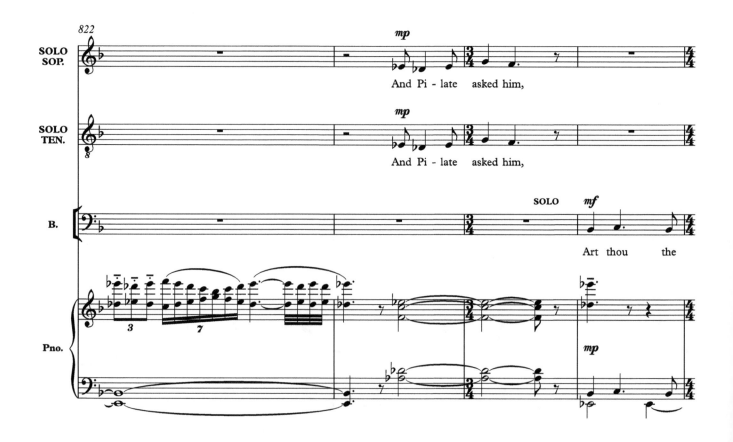

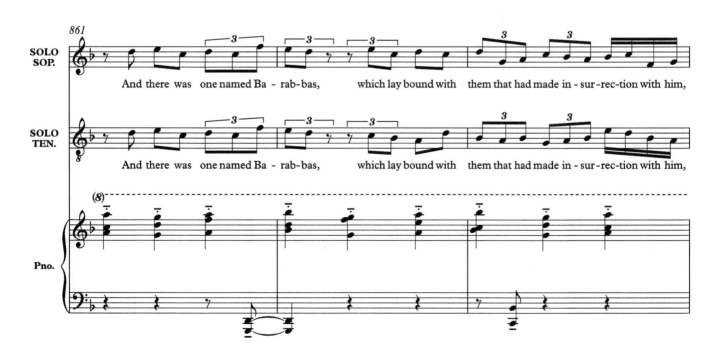

SOLO SOP.
For he knew that the chief priests had de - li - vered him for en - vy.

SOLO TEN.
For he knew that the chief priests had de - li - vered him for en - vy.

B.
King of the Jews?

But the chief priests moved the peo - ple, that he should ra - ther re - lease Ba - rab - bas un - to them.

But the chief priests moved the peo - ple, that he should ra - ther re - lease Ba - rab - bas un - to them.

And Pi - late an - swered and said a - gain un - to them,

And Pi - late an - swered and said a - gain un - to them,

6. Crucifixion

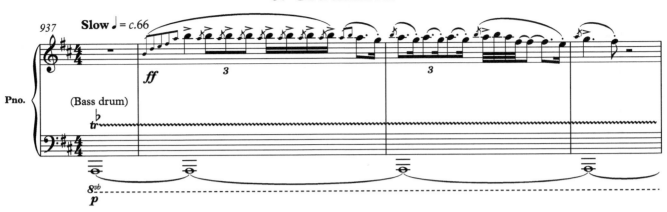

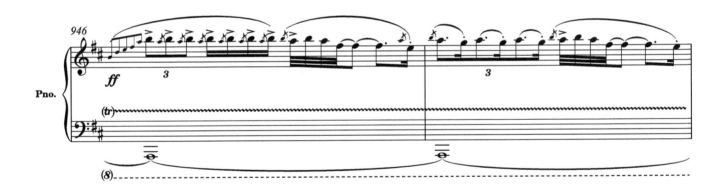

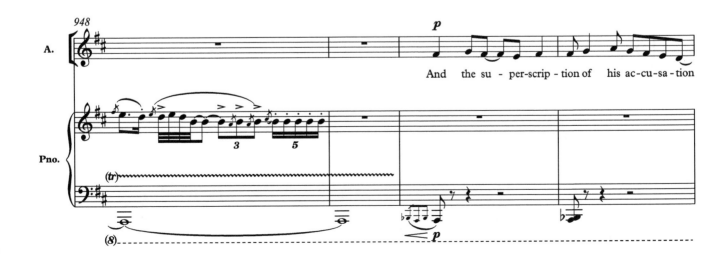

when they heard it,___ said, Be - hold,___ he call - eth E - li - as.___

Be - hold,___ he call - eth E - li - as.___

And one ran and filled a spunge full of vi - ne - gar, and put it on a reed,

and gave him___ to drink, say - ing,___

Let a - lone;___ let us see whe-ther E -li - as___ will come to take him

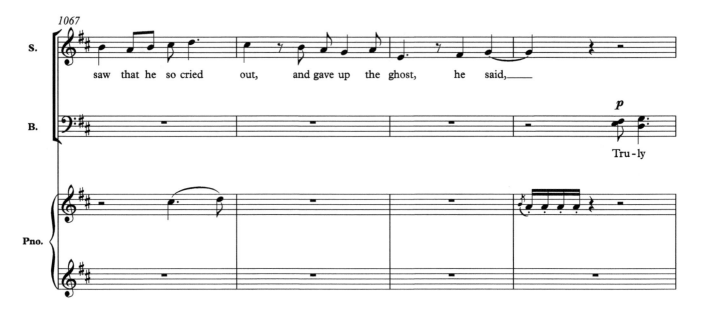

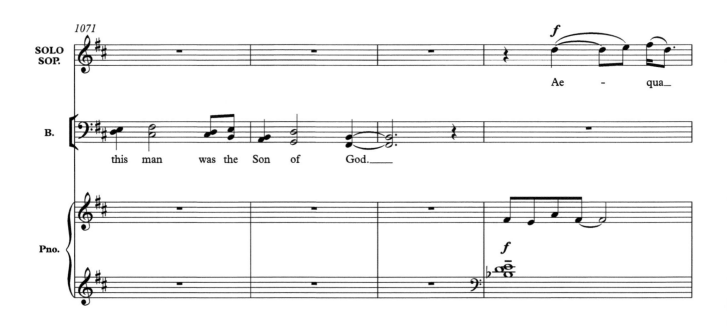

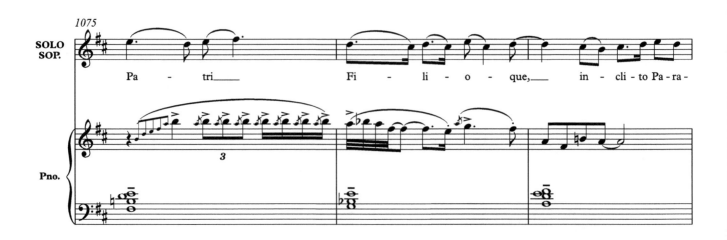

7. The End and the Beginning

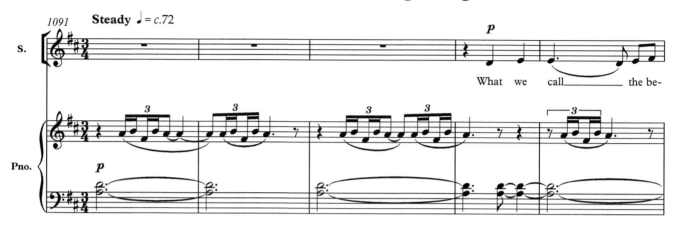

124

re - mem-bered gate_____ When the last of earth_____

left_____ to dis - co - ver Is that_____ which was_____ the be - gin -

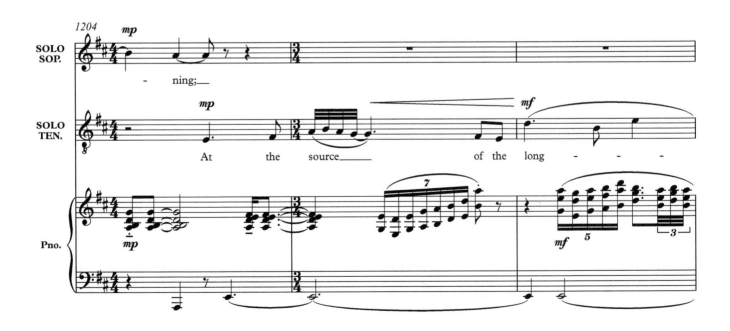

-ning;_____

At the source_____ of the long - - -

The voice_____ of the hid -

- est ri - - ver

- den wa - - - - - - - ter-fall

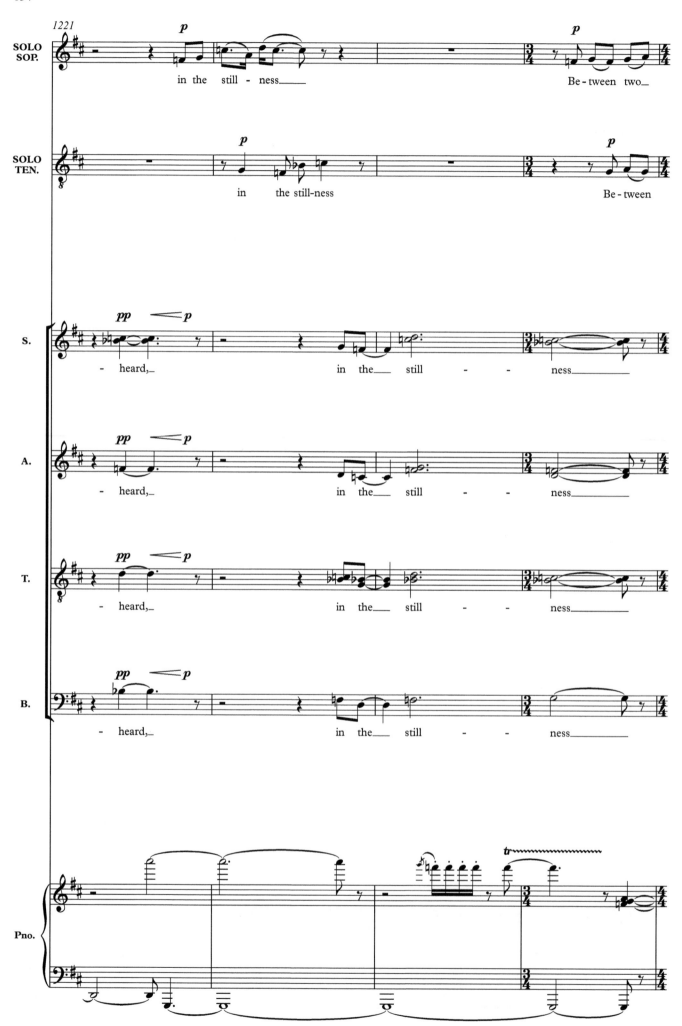

Brockley, April 2013–February 2014